FALL
IS FUN!

by Walt K. Moon

LERNER PUBLICATIONS ◆ MINNEAPOLIS

Note to Educators:

Throughout this book, you'll find critical thinking questions. These can be used to engage young readers in thinking critically about the topic and in using the text and photos to do so.

Lerner Publications Company
A division of Lerner Publishing Group, Inc.
241 First Avenue North
Minneapolis, MN 55401 USA

For reading levels and more information, look up this title at www.lernerbooks.com.

Library of Congress Cataloging-in-Publication Data

Names: Moon, Walt K., author.
Title: Fall is fun! / by Walt K. Moon.
Description: Minneapolis : Lerner Publications, [2017] | Series: Bumba books—Season fun | Audience: Ages 4–8. | Audience: K to grade 3. | Includes bibliographical references and index.
Identifiers: LCCN 2015048803 (print) | LCCN 2016001470 (ebook) | ISBN 9781512414097 (lb : alk. paper) | ISBN 9781512415292 (pb : alk. paper) | ISBN 9781512415308 (eb pdf)
Subjects: LCSH: Autumn—Juvenile literature. | Seasons—Juvenile literature.
Classification: LCC QB637.7 .M66 2017 (print) | LCC QB637.7 (ebook) | DDC 508.2—dc23

LC record available at http://lccn.loc.gov/2015048803

Manufactured in the United States of America
1 – VP – 7/15/16

LERNER
SOURCE

Expand learning beyond the printed book. Download free, complementary educational resources for this book from our website, www.lernerresource.com.

Table of Contents

Fall Season

Each year has four seasons.

Fall is one season.

Temperatures cool down in fall.

Fall comes after the hot summer.

The days get shorter.

The sun sets earlier.

Leaves change colors.

They turn yellow, orange, and red.

Then they fall.

Why do you think leaves change color?

Farmers harvest their crops. They gather corn and other foods from fields.

Why do you think farmers harvest their crops in fall?

It will be cold soon.

Some animals hide food.

A squirrel stores a nut.

It will eat the nut in winter.

Why do animals store food for the winter?

Many birds fly south.

They find warmer weather.

Fall holidays are fun.

People celebrate Halloween.

They eat a big meal for Thanksgiving.

Fall is a beautiful season.

People walk through a forest.

They look at changing leaves.

Summer vacation ends

in fall.

Kids go back to school.

What do you do in fall?

Seasons Cycle

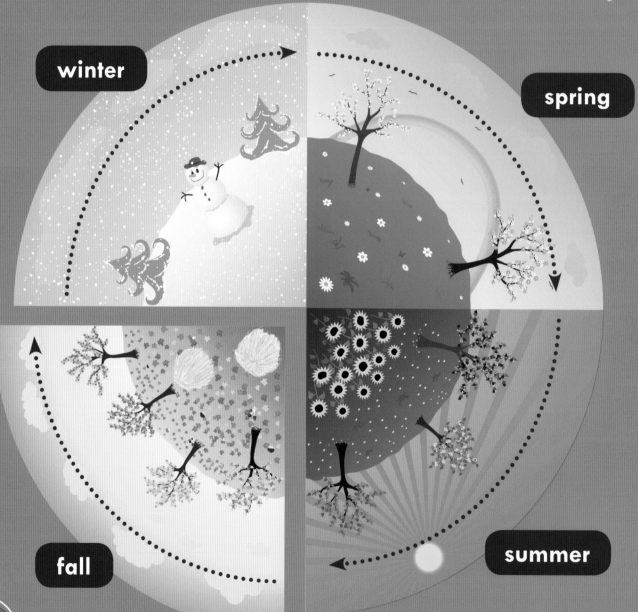

winter

spring

fall

summer

Picture Glossary

 crops

plants grown for food or goods

forest

a large area covered with full-grown trees

harvest

to gather crops from a field

leaves

flat structures with stems that grow from a branch

23

Index

Read More

Felix, Rebecca. *How's the Weather in Fall?* Ann Arbor, MI: Cherry Lake Publishing, 2013.

Herrington, Lisa M. *How Do You Know It's Fall?* New York: Children's Press, 2014.

Nelson, Robin. *Seasons.* Minneapolis: Lerner Publications, 2011.

Photo Credits